Who's Who in Mexican Government

Edited by **Marvin Alisky**

Center for Latin American Studies

ARIZONA STATE UNIVERSITY

Who's Who in Mexican Government

Edited by

Marvin Alisky
Arizona State University

Published by the

**Center for Latin American Studies
of Arizona State University**
Tempe, Arizona 85281
1969

INTRODUCTION

Not since 1946 when Stanford University brought one out has any institution in the United States published a Who's Who for Mexico and even textbooks on Mexican government do not include the biographical data which traces the rise up the public administration or political ladder of many Mexican leaders.

As Professor L. Vincent Padgett observed in his *Mexican Political System* (1966): "The person who is considered available for the presidency usually has been a cabinet officer." Lázaro Cárdenas (President 1934-1940) had been Minister of War. Manuel Avila Camacho (President 1940-1946) was Minister of Defense before his nomination as chief executive. Presidents Miguel Alemán (1946-1952), Adolfo Ruíz Cortines (1952-1958), and Gustavo Díaz Ordaz (1964-1970) had served in presidential cabinets as Minister of Gobernación (Interior). President Adolfo López Mateos became a presidential candidate for the 1958-1964 term after serving as Minister of Labor during 1952-1958.

If one looks a bit earlier in the careers of presidents, cabinet ministers, ambassadors, and other top-level public administrators of Mexico, usually one finds their experience included being governor or mayor or state supreme court justice, and almost invariably federal Deputy and then Senator.

As I pointed out in my monograph *Governors of Mexico* (1965), since the overthrow of the Porfirio Díaz dictatorship in 1911, most presidents have served as governors of their home states, gaining the experience which helped them serve in the cabinets of their presidential predecessors. President Carranza had been Governor of Coahuila. Presidents de la Huerta, Obregón, Calles, and Albelardo Rodríguez were Governors of Sonora. President Portes Gil had been Governor of Tamaulipas. Presidents Ortiz Rubio and Cárdenas were Governors of Michoacán. Presidents Alemán and Ruiz Cortines were Governors of Veracruz.

On occasion, a former Governor will become a Senator — almost never a Deputy in the lower house of the federal Congress — for the first time. But usually in Mexico one goes from Senator to Governor. Cabinet Ministers come as often from the ranks of the Senate as from the Governorships. And several Ministers, after serving their six years in the cabinet, then receive the majority party nomination for Governor of their home state.

For North American students of the Mexican political system, biographical data in organized form in English has been needed to bring into focus the career paths of Mexico's leaders. Merely studying the legal norms or the general theories will not bring insight into the system as it operates. For any political system is composed of functioning individuals, and these individuals must be analyzed in their political roles.

Despite many books in English on Mexican government and politics, one searches long for specific biographical data organized chronologically. Hence, the ASU Center for Latin American Studies makes available to students of Mexican public affairs full sketches of some prominent Mexican leaders, briefer resumes of others, and the briefest listings for still others.

Much of the data is taken from news stories from the leading Mexican newspapers and magazines, such as *Excélsior, Novedades, El Universal, and El Nacional* among the dailies; *Tiempo, Hoy, Siempre, Mañana,* and *Life En Español* among the magazines. Also consulted were the reference files of XEW and XEW-TV radio and television news, and the press officers of the cabinet ministries.

In some instances, the listee himself kindly confirmed by letter the biographical data but neither time nor funds permitted this in the case of all those listed.

Special thanks goes to Víctor M. Pesqueira, Consul of Mexico in Phoenix, Arizona; to the staff of Mexican Ambassador to the United States Hugo B. Margáin in Washington, D.C.; to the librarians at the Colégio de México; and to the faculty of the School of Political and Social Sciences of the National Autonomous University of Mexico.

Any errors are the sole responsibility of the editor. I alone condensed all the data into the available printed space.

If this *Who's Who in Mexican Government* proves to be as useful to researchers as I hope, the Center may then try to complete a similar guide for other Latin American republics. Already I have a skeleton manuscript for Peru and for Uruguay, and some data on leading officials in Central America. Your response to this pioneering effort on Mexico will help attract the funds and encourage the assignment of scarce time to complete similar guides for other Latin American nations, should that response be what we hope.

Marvin Alisky
Director, Center for Latin American Studies
Professor of Political Science

Arizona State University
Tempe, Arizona
January 1969

Abbreviations Used in this Directory:

PRI: Partido Revolucionario Institucional, the ruling Institutional Revolutionary Party of Mexico. Founded in 1929 as the PNR or National Revolutionary Party, in 1938 the name was changed to the PRM or Mexican Revolutionary Party. In 1946 the PRM became the PRI.

PAN: Partido de Acción Nacional, the principal minority party, the National Action Party, to the political right of the PRI.

PPS: Partido Popular Socialista, the Popular Socialist Party, to the political left of the PRI.

UNAM: Universidad Nacional Autonónoma de México, the National Autonomous University of Mexico.

Rather than struggle with social perspective in going from Spanish into English from the Mexican to the North American cultural norms, the biographies have not used the term "Licenciado," which denotes a degree in law or in economics. Rather the term "law degree" has been used in the sketches. For Mexicans with the title of "Dr.," designations have been made as to medical, dental, and earned Ph.D degrees.

The custom of misusing the title "Dr." for a law degree so common in Latin America is not used often in Mexico. Some of the listees has the title "Ing.," indicating either a degree in engineering or in agronomy. The specific specialty was determined and listed instead of the title.

4

A

ABARCA Alarcón, Raymundo. Born in Guerrero. Medical degree. Active in public health work. Nominated by the PRI and elected in 1962 Governor of the state of Guerrero for the term April 1, 1963 to April 1, 1969.

ACEVES Parra, Salvador. Medical degree. PRI campaigner. Undersecretary of Public Health. Acting Minister of Public Health. On October 22, 1968, appointed Minister of Public Health in the cabinet of President Díaz Ordaz for a term ending December 1, 1970.

ACOSTA, Ricardo. Engineering agronomy degree. Active in PRI. Undersecretary of Agriculture in the cabinet of President Díaz Ordaz 1964-1970.

ACOSTA Romo, Fausto. Born in Sonora. Law degree. Practicing attorney. PRI campaigner. Official of the National Bank for Communal-Farm (Ejido) Credit in Ciudad Obregón. Assistant Attorney General for the federal government. Acting Governor of Sonora August-September 1951. Senator from Sonora 1952-1958. Unsuccessful candidate for PRI nomination for Governor of Sonora in 1961 and 1967.

AGUILAR Castillo, Magdaleno. Born in Tamaulipas. PRI campaigner. Senator from Tamaulipas 1964-1970.

AGUIRRE, Manuel Bernardo. Born in Chihuahua in 1907. Campaign youth director for the state of Chihuahua for the election of President Plutarco Elías Calles in 1924. Mayor of the municipality of Chihuahua City. Federal Deputy from Chihuahua. Secretary for Political Action of the National Executive Committee (CEN) of the PRI. Nominated by the PRI in 1964 and elected Senator from Chihuahua for the 1964-1970 term. In 1967 chosen chairman of the Gran Comisión of the Senate.

AGUIRRE, Norberto. Engineering agronomy degree. Appointed by President Díaz Ordaz in December 1964 as Director of the Department of Agrarian Affairs and Colonization (DAAC) to deal with land reform and communal-farm (ejido) problems.

ALCALA de Lira, Alberto. Born in Aguascalientes. Active in the PRI at the municipal and state levels. Senator from Aguascalientes 1964-1970.

ALEMAN Valdés, Miguel. Born in Savula, Veracruz, on September 29, 1900, the son of General Miguel Alemán (1884-1929). Law degree from the National Autonomous University of Mexico in 1929. State Supreme Court Justice in Veracruz in 1935. Senator from Veracruz 1936. Elected Governor of Veracruz in 1936. Campaign manager for Presidential candidate Manuel Avila Camacho in 1939. Secretary of Gobernación 1940-1946. President of the Republic of Mexico from December 1, 1946 to December 1, 1952. Investment banker and corporation lawyer. Since 1964 director of the National Tourism Commission of the federal government. Head of conservative wing of the PRI, the Revolutionary Front of Civic Affirmation (FRAC).

ALVARADO, Silverio Ricardo. Federal District (D. F.) committeeman in the PRI. Federal Deputy from the 2nd congressional district of the Federal District, 1967-1970.

ALVAREZ Acosta, Miguel. Law degree from the National University of Mexico. Career diplomat. Ambassador and Director General of the Organization for the International Promotion of Culture (OPIC) of the Ministry of Foreign Relations, 1964-1970.

ALVAREZ Amézquita, José. Medical degree. Practicing physician. Secretary of Public Health and Welfare in the cabinet of President López Mateos, 1958-1964.

ALVAREZ Borboa, Teófilo. Born in Sinaloa. Career officer, Army; retired as Division General. Senator from Sinaloa, 1958-1964.

ALVAREZ González, Manuel. Member of PRI campaign team in the D. F. in 1964 and 1967. Federal Deputy from the 10th congressional district of the Federal District, 1967-1970.

ARELLANO Tapia, Alicia. Born in Magdalena, Sonora. Degree in dentistry. Directed free dental clinic services for the indigent under the PRI welfare program. Elected Federal Deputy from Sonora in 1963. Elected Senator from Sonora for 1964-1970, one of the first two women ever elected to the Mexican Senate.

ARNAIZ y Freg, Arturo. Director of Public Relations for the Ministry of Communications 1958-1964. Director of Public Relations for the Mexican Institute of Social Security 1964-1970. Professor of history at the National University. Author of books on Juárez.

ARRIAGA Rivera, Agustín. Born in Michoacán in 1925. Bachelor's degree from Morelia Preparatory College. Economics degree. Professor at the Universities of Michoacán and of Tamaulipas. Federal Deputy from the 3rd congressional district of Michoacán. Chairman of the Junta de Mejoras Materiales (Federal Betterment Board) of Nuevo Laredo, Tamaulipas 1955-1959. Governor of the state of Michoacán from September 16, 1962 to September 16, 1968.

ARROYO Ch., Agustín. Born in Guanajuato. Director of the Autonomous Department of Press and Publicity (DAPP) under President Cárdenas during 1934-1940. Publisher of the government's daily newspaper, *El Nacional* from April 1962 to January 1968. Board member of PIPSA, governmental import-export paper agency 1967-1969.

B

BADILLO Ortiz, Gonzalo. Born in Hidalgo. PRI campaigner. Federal Deputy from the 4th congressional district of Hidalgo, 1967-1970.

BALBOA Gojón, Praxedis. Born in Ciudad Victoria, Tamaulipas. Preparatory School at the Colegio Civil in Monterrey, Nuevo León.

Law degree from the National University of Mexico in August 1925. Federal conciliator for Railroad Mixed Commission in 1929. Federal Deputy from Tampico 1930. Federal Deputy from Tampico 1934-1937. Assistant Director of Petroleos Mexicanos 1952-1958. Nominated by the PRI as Governor of the State of Tamaulipas in 1962, and elected for the term 1963-1969.

BARRAGAN, Manuel L. Born in Nuevo León in 1888. Writer and newspaper columnist. Investor and financier. Industrialist. State committeeman of the PRI in Nuevo León. Member of the Board of Regents of the state University of Nuevo León. In September 1968, at age 80, wrote report on public service responsibilities of governmental officials.

BARRERA Fuentes, Federico. Career diplomat. Since 1968 Mexican Ambassador to the Philippines.

BARROS Sierra, Javier. Engineering degree. Grandson of organizer of the revived National University, Justo Sierra. Secretary of Public Works in the cabinet of President López Mateos during 1958-1964. President of the National Autonomous University of Mexico (UNAM), 1965-1969.

BAZ, Gustavo. Medical degree. Originator of clinics operated by the Revolutionary Party in 1936. Secretary of Public Health and Welfare in the cabinet of President Avila Camacho during 1940-1946. Governor of the state of México during 1957-1963. Chairman of the Trust Fund of the Hospital de Jesús, serving workers not covered by Social Security, 1964-1970.

BELLO Bobadilla, Antonio. Law degree. Former justice of the Supreme Court of the state of Guerrero. Publisher of the magazine *Revista de Información Petrolera,* distributed to employees of the governmental agency Pemex.

BERLIN Valenzuela, Francisco. Born in Jalapa, Veracruz, in 1940. Law degree at the National University of Mexico. Instructor in civics and Mexican history. Founder of the Public Speaking Ateneo of the Law School of the UNAM. Chief of the Public Relations Office of the Mexican Institute of Social Security. On August 24, 1967, was appointed director of the Youth Division of the PRI.

BERMUDEZ, Antonio J. Veteran public administrator. Director of Petroleos Mexicanos, the government oil-industry agency. Director of the National Border Development Program (Programa Nacional Fronterizo) along the United States border since 1961.

BERRUETO Ramón, Federico. Professor at secondary schools in Coahuila. Educational administrator for the state of Coahuila. State committeeman of the PRI in Coahuila. Senator from Coahuila for the term 1958-1964. In 1964, educational consultant for political action groups. Assistant Secretary of Public Education in the cabinet of President Díaz, 1964-1970.

BLANCO Sánchez, Javier. Committeeman for the PAN in the Federal District. Federal Deputy from the congressional district of the Federal District, 1967-1970.

BOBADILLA, Manuel R. Born in Sonora. Youth Committee of the PRI. Federal Deputy from the 3rd congressional district of Sonora, 1964-1967.

BONILLA Vázquez, Ignacio. Born in Tlaxcala. Career officer in the Army. Brigadier General, retired. Senator from Tlaxcala from September 1964 to July 1968. Nominated by the PRI for Governor of the state of Tlaxcala in August 1968. Elected October 27, 1968, for the term 1969 to 1975.

BRAVO Ahuja, Victor. Born in Oaxaca. Educator. Director of Summer Sessions, Monterrey Institute of Technology, 1951-55. General

Administrator, MIT. Undersecretary of Education, federal Ministry of Public Education, in charge of vocational and technical education. Elected on August 4, 1968, Governor of the state of Oaxaca for the term December 1, 1968 to December 1, 1974.

BRAVO Izquierdo, Donato. Born in Puebla. Career officer, Army. Division General, retired. Senator from Puebla for the term 1958-1964.

BRENA Torres, Rodolfo. Born in Ejutla, Oaxaca, on May 16, 1911. Law degree from the National University of Mexico. Practicing attorney in Mexico City, specializing in labor law. Senator from Oaxaca during 1958-1964, serving as president of the Gran Comisión of the Senate, chairman of the Senate Foreign Trade Committee, then chairman of the Senate Labor Committee. In 1959 Mexican delegate to the Organization of American States economic commission. Mexican delegate to the OAS Foreign Ministers Conference in 1960 and 1962. Elected Governor of the state of Oaxaca in 1962 for the term December 1, 1962 to December 1, 1968.

BURROLA Tolano, Jesús. Born in Sonora. Elected Mayor of the municipality of Cananea, Sonora, July 2, 1961, as the PPS candidate, upsetting the PRI favorite. Publisher of the weekly organ of Section 65 of the National Miners Union, the Sindicato Minero Nacional.

C

CAMPOS Salas, Octavio. Born in San Luis Potosí in 1916. Teacher at a Normal School. Economics degree. Graduate study in economics in universities in the U. S. Director of the Institute of Political, Economic, and Social Studies of the PRI. President of the Colegio de Economistas de México. Professor of economics, National Autonomous University of Mexico. Dean of the National School of Economics of the National University. General coordinator of programs of the PRI during the 1964 presidential campaign of Gustavo Díaz Ordaz. Author of various books on economics. Secretary of Industry and Commerce in the cabinet of President Díaz Ordaz during 1964-1970.

CARDENAS, Lázaro. Born in Jiquilpán de Juárez, Michoacán on May 21, 1895. Joined the revolutionary forces in 1913. Appointed captain in the Revolutionary Army 1914. Colonel commanding 22nd Regiment 1915. Brigadier General 1924. Division General 1928. Provisional Governor of the state of Michoacán 1920, constitutional Governor of Michoacán 1928-1932. President of the National Revolutionary Party (now the PRI) 1930. Secretary of War and Navy 1933. President of the Republic of Mexico from December 1, 1934 to December 1, 1940. Special wartime service as Minister of National Defense during 1943-1946. In December 1961 became director of the Río Balsas Commission, to expand hydroelectric projects. In 1964 was chairman of the committee for the Study of New Politics of the National Liberation Movement (MLN). In 1968 denounced MLN rioters.

CARRILLO, Alejandro. Elementary education in San Antonio, Texas, where his father was consul general of Mexico. Student Tulane University. Publisher of leftist-labor daily newspaper *El Popular* from 1938 to 1945. General Secretary of Workers University. Secretary of the government of the Federal District. Secretary of the National Committee of the Mexican Federation of Labor. (CTM). Mexican Ambassador to the United Arab Republic. Chief negotiator of the Mexican committee bidding for the 1968 Olympic Games at the 1963 meeting of the International Olympic Committee. Federal Deputy in Congress, 1964-1967. Professor at the National Preparatory School and Dean of the History Faculty at the Mexican Superior War College, 1968-1969. On January 18, 1968, named publisher of the government's daily newspaper, *El Nacional*.

CARRILLO FLORES, Antonio. Born in Mexico City on June 23, 1909. Law degree from the National University of Mexico. Professor of law, National Autonomous University 1944, and Dean of the School of Law 1945. Honorary Doctor of Laws degree from UNAM 1949. Administrator, governmental lending agency Nacional Financiera, beginning in October 1945. Secretary of Finance and Public Credit in the cabinet of President Ruíz Cortines 1952-1958. Mexican Ambassador to the United States, December 1958 to December 1964. Secretary of Foreign Relations in the cabinet of President Díaz Ordaz during 1964-1970.

CARVAJAL, Angel. Law degree. PRI campaigner. Secretary of Gobernación in the cabinet of President Ruíz Cortines during 1952-1958. Justice of the federal Supreme Court.

CASTILLO Ledón, Amalia. Founder of the Mexican Alliance of Women. President Revolutionary Federation of Women. National Committeewoman of the PRI. In 1953 became the first woman to address the Senate of Mexico on the new law to give women full political rights and suffrage. President of the Inter-American Commission of Women under Organization of American States auspices. First woman diplomat in Mexico to achieve rank of ambassador, serving since 1956 as Mexican Ambassador to Sweden, then Mexican Ambassador to Switzerland, then adviser to the Minister of Foreign Relations. First woman to become part of the cabinet of a Mexican president, when appointed Undersecretary of Public Education in the cabinet of President López Mateos from December 1958 to December 1964.

CASTILLO Mena, Ignacio. Law degree. Press officer for the Ministry of Industry and Commerce, 1964-1970.

CASTILLO Tielemans, José. Born in Chiapas. Law degree. Municipal committeeman of the PRI in Tuxla Gutiérrez. Senator from Chiapas from September 1958 through April 1964. In May 1964 was nominated by the PRI for Governor of the state of Chiapas, and elected for the term December 1, 1964 to December 1, 1970.

CASTRO Elías, Miguel. Born in Veracruz. Active in PRI campaigns. Federal Deputy from the 9th congressional district of Veracruz, 1964-1967.

CASTRO Estrada, José. Law degree. Practicing attorney. Justice of the federal Supreme Court.

CASTRO Sánchez, Juventino. Born in Querétaro. Accounting degree. PRI campaigner. Governor of the state of Querétaro for the term from September 1968 to September 1974.

CERVANTES del Río, Hugo. Law degree. Practicing attorney. Director of the Federal Commission for Roads and Bridges, 1964-1965. Appointed Governor of the federal Territory of Baja California Sur in May 1965 for the term 1965-1970.

CERVANTES Hernández, Anselmo. Law degree. Active in PRI campaigns. Governor of the state of Tlaxcala for the term January 15, 1963 to January 15, 1969.

CHRISTLIEB Ibarrola, Adolfo. Born in Mexico City on March 12, 1919. Law degree from the National University in 1941. Joined the PAN in 1942, serving as counselor for the party, member of the PAN executive committee, and PAN representative for the Federal Electoral Commission. Federal Deputy during 1964-1967. President of the PAN from November 1962 to September 1968.

CONTRERAS Martínez, María de los Angeles. Leader of women's groups of the PRI in the state of Guanajuato. Federal Deputy from the 7th congressional district of Guanajuato, 1967-1970.

CORREA, Víctor. PAN leader in the state of Yucatán. Mayor of Mérida 1968 to 1971.

CORONA del Rosal, Alfonso. Graduate of the National Military College, commissioned a lieutenant of cavalry. Promoted to Colonel, then Brigadier General. Law degree from the National Autonomous University. Degree in biology. Professor of labor law at the National Military College. Federal Deputy from Hidalgo. Senator from Hidalgo. General Manager of the Army-Navy Bank. Governor of the state of Hidalgo. President of the National Executive Patrimony in the cabinet of President Díaz Ordaz from December 1964 to September 1966. Governor of the Federal District 1966-1970.

CORRAL Camou, Alejandro. Born September 26, 1930, in Hermosillo, Sonora. Graduate of American Primary School in Mexico City. Student at the Free School of Law. Became leader in the Nationalist Party of Mexico (PNM) in 1959, and PNM Secretary General in February 1961. By 1964 this conservative party had been dissolved. Leader of rightwing political action groups.

CRAVIOTO Cisneros, Oswaldo. Born in Hidalgo. Army officer, reverting to inactive duty as a Major. Active in the PRI. Senator from Hidalgo 1964-1970.

CUE Merlo, Eduardo. Born in Puebla. Active in the PRI. Senator from Puebla 1964-1970.

CUETO Ramírez, Luis. Career officer in the Army. Advanced study of military police administration. Brigadier General, returned to inactive status to become police administrator. Chief of police of the Federal District 1961-1969.

D

DARIO Ojeda, Carlos. Law degree. Executive Officer (Oficial Mayor) for the Ministry of Foreign Relations during 1964-1970.

DE LA VEGA Domínguez, Jorge. Born in Chipas in 1931. Economics degree. Assistant Director of Diesel Nacional Truck Company. Federal Deputy to Congress. Active in PRI. Professor economics at the National Polytechnical Institute. On August 5, 1968, elected president of the Institute of Political, Economic, and Social Education of the PRI.

DE LARA, Alfredo. Born in Aguascalientes. Law degree. PRI campaigner. Senator from Aguascalientes 1958-1964.

DIAZ Ordaz, Gustavo. Born in San Andrés, Puebla, in 1911. Law degree from the National University of Mexico. Became a practicing attorney in February 1937. Prosecuting Attorney for the Municipality of Tehuacán, Puebla. Criminal District Court Judge in Puebla. Director of the Labor-Management Conciliation Board in Puebla. Justice of the state Supreme Court of Puebla. Federal Deputy to Congress. Professor of Law University of Puebla. Senator from Puebla 1946 to 1952. Chief Administrative Officer, then Executive Officer (Oficial Mayor) of the Ministry of Gobernación, 1952-1958. Minister of Gobernación in the cabinet of President López Mateos 1958-to 1964. President of Mexico from December 1964 to December 1970.

DOMENE, Juan Manuel. PRI campaigner. Executive Officer (Oficial Mayor) for the office of the Presidency during the administration of President Díaz Ordaz, 1964-1970.

DUPRE Ceniceros, Enrique. Engineering degree. Senator from Durango 1958-1964. Nominated by the PRI and elected Governor of Durango for the term September 15, 1962 to September 15, 1968. Resigned the governorship August 4, 1966. Became inactive in the PRI.

E

ECHEVERRIA Alvarez, Luis. Born in 1922. Law degree from the National Autonomous University of Mexico. Platform adviser for the PRI in 1946. Administrator in the Ministry of the Navy. Undersecretary of Gobernación from December 1958 to November 1963. Acting Secretary of Gobernación in the cabinet of President Díaz Ordaz for the term 1964 to 1970.

ELIAS Romero, Leopoldo. Born in Tijuana, Baja California, in 1912. Secondary School in Nogales, Sonora. National University of Mexico economics. Teller with the Banco de Londres y México. Inspector in customs. President of the Regional Cattlemen's Association of Sonora. Active in the PRI since 1940. Former member of the Federal Betterment Board of Nogales. Mayor of Nogales, Sonora, for the term 1967-1970.

ELIZONDO, Eduardo A. Law degree. Nominated by the PRI and elected Governor of the state of Nuevo León for the term October 4, 1967 to October 4, 1973.

ENCINAS Johnson, Luis. Law degree. Practicing Attorney. Representative in the state Legislature of Sonora 1955-1958. President of the University of Sonora. Governor of the state of Sonora for the term September 1, 1961 to September 1, 1967.

ESPINOSA, Fernando. Engineering degree. Undersecretary of Public Works in the cabinet of President Díaz Ordaz during 1964-1970.

ESPINOZA, José. Certified Public Accountant. Secretary of Finances for the Institutional Revolutionary Party (PRI) since 1964.

ESPINOZA de los Reyes, Jorge. Law degree. Assistant Director of Petróleos Mexicanos, governmental oil agency, during 1964-1970.

ESTRADA Rodríguez, Amado. Law degree. Senator from Sinalóa during 1964-1970.

F

FABELA, Ramón. Engineering degree. Active in PRI. Executive Officer (Oficial Mayor) for the Ministry of Communications and Transportation in the cabinet of President Díaz Ordaz 1964-1970.

FARIAS, Luis M. Born in Nuevo León. Law degree. Radio announcer in Monterrey. Executive Officer (Oficial Mayor) for the federal Tourism Commission. Federal Deputy from Nuevo León during 1967-1970 and PRI majority leader in the lower house of Congress. Chairman of the Permanent Commission of Congress for 1967-1970.

FELIX Serna, Faustino. Born in Sonora in 1913. Rancher and official in Cattlemen's Association. Mayor of Cuidad Obregón 1961-1963. Federal Deputy from southern congressional district of Sonora 1964-1967. Nominated by the PRI and elected in 1967 as Governor of Sonora for the term September 1967 to September 1973.

FERNANDEZ Aguirre, Braulio. Federal Deputy from Coahuila 1961-1963. Resigned before congressional term ended when nominated by the PRI in 1963 for Governor of Coahuila; elected for the term December 1, 1963 to December 1, 1969.

FERNANDEZ Albarrán, Juan. Born in the state of México. Law degree. PRI committeeman from Toluca. Governor of the state of México September 16, 1963 to September 16, 1969.

FLORES, Oscar. Born in Chihuahua. Active in PRI. Governor of the state of Chihuahua October 4, 1968 to October 4, 1974.

FLORES Mazari, Antonio. Senator from Morelos 1964-1970.

FRAGA, Gambino. University professor. Author of *El Municipio en México* 1943. Undersecretary of Foreign Relations in the cabinet of President Díaz Ordaz 1964-1970.

FRANCO Bencomo, Joaquín. Engineering degree. Secretary General of New Communal-Farm (Ejido) Affairs in the federal Department of Agrarian Affairs and Colonization, 1965-1969.

G

GALINDO Ochoa, Francisco. Press Secretary for President Díaz Ordaz 1964-1970.

GALVAN, Rafael. Born in Michoacán. PRI state committeeman. Senator from Michoacán 1964-1970.

GALVEZ Betancourt, Carlos. Law degree. Undersecretary of Gobernación 1964-1968. Nominated by PRI as Governor of Michoacán, elected for the term September 16, 1968 to September 16, 1974.

GANDARA, César. Born in Sonora. Owner of hotels and motels. President of the National Association of Hotels of Mexico. Mayor of Hermosillo, Sonora, 1958-1961. Secretary of State under Governor Félix for 1967-1973.

GASCON Mercado, Julián. Born in Tepic, Nayarit, on January 28, 1925. Son of peasant farmers, he won a campesino scholarship to the Tepic Secondary School. Medical degree from the National University of Mexico. Director of the UNAM Hospital. Official in the National Federation of Peasant-Farmers (CNC). Nominated by the PRI and elected in 1963 as Governor of Nayarit for the term January 1, 1964 to January 1, 1970.

GIL Preciado, Juan. Born in Juchitlán, Jalisco on June 26, 1909. Bachelor's degree from Guadalajara International College. Education degree in secondary education. Principal of the Secondary School of Ocotlán, Jalisco 1927-1928. Major in the 32nd Regiment of the Army as professor of civics in 1929. Secretary General of the Polytechnical School of the University of Guadalajara and Professor of Mathematics. Executive Secretary for General Ruperto García de Alba, Governor of the Territory of Baja California Sur. Executive Officer (Oficial Mayor) for the Territory of Baja California Sur. Director of Extension for the University of Guadalajara in 1936. PRI Committee chairman for Guadalajara in 1938. Federal Deputy to Congress from Jalisco 1940-1943. Director of Planning for the federal Agrarian Department in 1943. Director of Information for the U.S.-Mexican Mixed Commission on Hoof-and-Mouth Disease in 1947. Federal Deputy from Jalisco 1953. Mayor of Guadalajara 1956-1959. Governor of Jalisco 1959-1964. Secretary of Agriculture in the cabinet of President Díaz Ordaz 1964-1970.

GINER Durán, Praxedes. Born in Camargo, Chihuahua, on February 15, 1893. Joined the Revolutionary Forces in 1911, rising through the ranks to Division General. Chief of military operations for the various army divisions in successive assignments. Governor of the state of Chihuahua October 1962 to October 1968.

GOMEZ Villanueva, Augusto. Law degree. In October 1967 elected Secretary General of the National Federation of Peasant-Farmers, Confederación Nacional de Campesinos (CNC).

GOMEZ Sada, Napoleón. Born in Nuevo León. Active in PRI. Senator from Nuevo León 1964-1970.

GOMEZ Zepeda, Luis. Born in Aguascalientes. Senator from Aguascalientes 1964-1970.

GONZALES Aparicio, Luis. Degree in architecture. Senator from the Federal District 1964-1970.

GONZALES Blanco, Alberto. Law degree. Practicing attorney. Justice of the federal Supreme Court since 1964.

GONZALES Blanco, Salomón. Law degree. Minister of Labor in the cabinet of President Díaz Ordaz 1964-1970.

GONZALES Bustamente, Juan José. Born in San Luis Potosí. Doctor's degree. Senator from San Luis Potosí 1964-1970.

GONZALES Cosío, Manuel. Engineering degree. Governor of the state of Querétaro during October 1, 1961 to October 1, 1967.

GONZALES Luna, Efraín. Co-founder of the National Action Party in 1939. Federal Deputy for minority-party seat in Congress. PAN candidate for President of Mexico in 1952.

GONZALES Ortiz, Guadalupe. Born in Coahuila. Leader of women's groups in the PRI. First woman elected to the state Legislature of Coahuila in 1962. Degree in education. Teacher. Leader in national women's groups in the PRI.

GONZALES Torres, José. PAN leader and campaigner. PAN candidate for President of Mexico in 1964.

GONZALES Varela, José. Medical degree. Military physician. Army General, PRI campaigner. Senator from Zacatecas 1964-1970.

GUTIERREZ Treviño, Eulalio. Born in Coahuila. Engineering degree. Active in PRI. Senator from Coahuila 1964-1970.

GUZMAN Cárdenas, Cristóbal. Born in Durango. Army officer, reverting to inactive status as General. PRI committeeman. Senator from Durango 1964-1970.

GUZMAN Orozco, Renaldo. Director of the National Federation of Popular Organizations (CNOP) of the PRI.

H

HANK González, Carlos. Education degree. Professor at preparatory schools. Public administrator. Since 1964 Director General of CONA-SUPO, the Compañía Nacional de Subsistencias Populares, a federal agency selling food and basic commodities to low-income groups.

HERNANDEZ, Amador. Administrator of **communal-farm** relations within the National Federation of Peasant-Farmers (CNC). Secretary General of the CNC 1966 until October 1967. Adviser to the PRI on party relations with the CNC 1968-1970.

HERNANDEZ Ochoa, Rafael. Law degree Active in the PRI. Under-secretary of Gobernación Ministry in the cabinet of President Díaz Ordaz during 1964-1970.

HERNANDEZ Terán, José. Engineering degree. Federal public administrator. Minister of Water Resources in the cabinet of President Díaz Ordaz during 1964-1970.

HOPKINS Duraz, Armando. Engineering degree. Speaker of the House of the state Legislature of Sonora 1961-1964. Director of Institute of Social Sciences Research of the University of Sonora. Active in the PRI. Director of Social Security for Government Employees in Sonora. Director of Development for the state of Sonora since September 1967.

HUERTA Sánchez, Luciano. Born in Tlaxcala. Medical degree. PRI committeeman. Senator from Tlaxcala during 1964-1970.

I

IBAÑEZ Llamas, Santiago. Law degree. PRI committeeman. Director General of the National Institute for the Protection of Children, a federal agency, during 1964-1970.

J

JIMENEZ Delgado, Ramón. Career officer in the Army. Reverted to inactive status as Brigadier General. Since 1964 Chief of the Federal Judicial Police, under the federal Attorney General.

L

LAMADRID, José Luis. Press secretary for the National Executive Committee of the PRI since 1964.

LANGLE Martínez, Eduardo. Law degree. Practicing attorney. Active in PRI. Assistant Attorney General for the Federal District and the two Federal Territories, 1964-1970.

LANZ Islas, Jorge. Career officer in the Navy. Vice Admiral, commander of the fleet, 1964-1970.

LARA Sosa, Héctor. Engineering degree. Professional petroleum engineer. Public administrator. Assistant Director of Petroleos Mexicanos, the government oil-industry entity, 1964-1970.

LAVALLE Urbina, María. Born in Campeche. Law degree. Attorney for labor unions. Leader of Feminine Action of the PRI 1957. Federal Deputy from Campeche. One of the first two women in Mexico elected to the Senate in 1964, as Senator from Campeche 1964-1970.

LAZO Hinojosa, César. Born in Nuevo León. Engineering degree. PRI committeeman in Monterrey. Elected in 1966 for a 3-year term as Mayor of Monterrey, Nuevo León.

LEYVA Mancilla, Baltasar R. Career officer in the Army. Reverted to inactive duty as Brigadier General. PRI committeeman in the state of Guerrero. Senator from Guerrero 1964-1970.

LIMON Muñoz, Jesús. Born in Jalisco. Law degree. Active in PRI. Secretary General of the state of Jalisco, 1959-1964.

LIVAS Villarreal, Eduardo. Born in Nuevo León. Law degree. Practicing attorney. Active in PRI. Governor of Nuevo León October 1961 to October 1967. Member of Board of Regents of University of Nuevo León.

LLORENTE González, Arturo. Born in Veracruz. Active in PRI. Law degree. Senator from Veracruz 1964-1970.

LOMBARDO Toledano, Vicente. Born in Teziutlán, Puebla, on July 16, 1894. Law degree at the National University of Mexico 1919. Doctor of Science in Jurisprudence, UNAM 1933. Professor at the Universidad Popular Mexicana 1917-1921. Professor of law, National University 1918-1933. Secretary of the government of the Federal District 1920. Director of Library of the Ministry of Public Education 1921. Director of the National Preparatory School of UNAM 1922-1923. Governor of the state of Puebla 1923. Federal Deputy in Congress 1926-1928. Secretary of the Regional Mexican Labor Federation (CROM). Founder of Labor University of Mexico 1934. A founder of the Mexican Federation of Labor (CTM) 1936. Publisher of the daily newspaper *El Popular* 1948. Founder of the Popular Socialist Party (PPS) 1948. Presidential Candidate of the PPS in 1952. Minority-Party seat member of Chamber of Deputies. Died on November 16, 1968 in Inglés Hospital in Mexico City.

LOPEZ, Josefina Caballero de. Born in Chihuahua. Married Sr. López. Education degree. Professor in secondary schools. Leader of Feminine Action of the PRI in Chihuahua. In 1962 elected Mayor of Chínipas, Chihuahua, as the state's first woman mayor.

LOPEZ Arias, Fernando. Born in Veracruz. Law degree. Practicing attorney. PRI committeeman for Veracruz. Senator from Veracruz. Federal Attorney General of Mexico 1958-1962. Governor of Veracruz from December 1962 to December 1968.

LOPEZ Dávila, Manuel. Education degree. Professor of secondary schools in San Luis Potosí. PRI committeeman. Education administrator San Luis Potosí. Governor of the state of San Luis Potosí from September 1961 to September 1967.

LOPEZ Guitiérrez, Francisco. Building contractor in Baja California. Municipal committeeman in Tijuana for the PRI. Mayor of Tijuana from December 1965 to December 1968.

LOPEZ Mateos, Adolfo. Born in Atizapán de Zaragoza, México, on May 26, 1910. Student Literary Institute of Toluca. Law degree from the National University of Mexico 1934. Secretary to Carlos Riva Palacio,President of the National Revolutionary Party 1931. Auditor of the Workers National Development Bank 1934. Chairman of the Publishing Committee of the Ministry of Education. Professor of History at the University of Toluca. A co-founder of the National School of Economics of the UNAM. Secretary General of the Union of Teachers. Senator from the state of México. Secretary General of the National Executive Committee of the PRI. Chairman of the Senate Foreign Relations Committee. Chief Mexican delegate to the International Economic Conference in Geneva 1951. Campaign manager for the PRI 1951. Member of the Federal Election Commission 1952. Minister of Labor in the Ruíz Cortines cabinet 1952-1958. President of Mexico December 1958 to December 1964. In a coma since May 1967 in Mexico City.

LOPEZ Mateos, Mariano. PRI youth committee. Director General of Almacenes Nacionales de Depósito (ANDSA), the federal agency for warehouse storage of basic commodities from CONASUPO (National Popular Subsistence Corporation), a companion federal entity, for the term 1964-1970.

LOPEZ Portilla, José. Born in Mexico City. Law student at the University of Chile in Santiago under a scholarship 1941-1945. Law degree. Graduate study in law at the National University of Mexico 1946-1950, for the doctorate in law. Professor of law at the UNAM 1948-1958. Director General of the Federal Material Betterment Boards (Juntas Federales de Mejoras Materiales) of border cities and ports of entry 1960. Legal Counsel for the Ministry of the Presidency 1965 to 1968. Undersecretary of the Ministry of the Presidency in the Díaz Ordaz cabinet from November 6, 1968 for a term ending December 1, 1970.

LORET de Mola, Carlos. Born in Yucatán. PRI committeeman for the state. Senator from Yucatáan for 1964-1970.

LOYO, Gilberto. Law degree. Economist. Minister of Economy (now Industry and Commerce) in the Ruíz Cortines cabinet 1952-1958. In

1968, Chairman of the Board of the Centro de Investigaciones Agrarias, semi-autonomous Agrarian Research Center founded in 1953 by the Food and Agricultural Organization of the UN and now linked to the Mexican Department of Agrarian Affairs and Colonization.

LOYOLA Zepeda, Jesús N. Born in San Luis Potosí. Medical degree. PRI state committeeman. Senator from San Luis Potosí for 1964-1970.

LUQUE Loyola, Eduardo. Born in Querétaro. Law degree. Active in PRI. Senator from Querétaro for 1964-1970.

M

MADRAZO, Carlos A. Born in Tabasco in 1915. Law degree. Professor of law at the National University. Governor of the state of Tabasco from 1959 into 1964. President of the PRI from December 1964 to December 1965. He brought the concept of a primary into the majority party in Chihuahua and Baja California, but the PRI National Executive Committee again rejected open regional contests for PRI nominations after Madrazo resigned as party president. In 1968 he became a prominent critic of the government regarding its handling of student protestors.

MAGRO Soto, Fernando. Law degree. Career public administrator. Director of the Postal Service of Mexico since 1964.

MALDONADO, Braulio. Law degree. First Governor of the state of Baja California Norte 1953-1959. Counselor for the Independent Peasant-Farmer Central (CCI) since 1966.

MARGAIN, Hugo B. Born in Mexico City on February 13, 1913. Law degree from the National University of Mexico in 1937. Professor of constitutional law at the UNAM in 1947. Professor of fiscal legislation at UNAM in 1952. Director General of federal Retail Merchants

Taxes in 1951. Director General of the federal Income Tax Bureau during 1952-1959. Executive Officer (Oficial Mayor) of the Ministry of Industry and Commerce from June 1959 to August 1961. Undersecretary of Industry and Commerce in the cabinet of President López Mateos from September 1961 to December 1964. Director of the National Commission of Profit Sharing 1963-1964. Since January 1, 1965, Mexican Ambassador to the United States.

MARTINEZ Domínguez, Alfonso. Born in Monterrey, Nuevo León, in 1922, direct descendant of Mexican leader Belisario Domínguez. Bachelor's degree from the Monterrey Franco-Mexican College. Clerk for the government of the Federal District 1935. Chief editor, Public Relations Department of the Federal District. Secretary General of the Section 15 Union of employees of the Federal District 1940-1943. Federal Deputy in Congress 1943-1946, 1952-1954, 1964-1967. Secretary General of the Federation of Unions of Government Employees (FSTSE), 1949-1953. Chairman of the U.S.-Mexican Interparliamentary Conference of Senators and Congressmen in La Paz, B.C., February 1965. President of the PRI and chairman of the National Executive Committee of the majority political party since 1966.

MARTINEZ Domínguez, Guillermo. Born in Monterrey in 1924, brother of Alfonso Martínez Domínguez. Orphaned at age 11, he was guided by his older brother through law school. Law degree. Practicing attorney. Director General of the Federal Electricity Commission (CFE).

MARTINEZ Manautou, Emilio. Doctor's degree from the National University. PRI committeeman. Secretary of the Ministry of the Presidency for Gustavo Díaz Ordaz during 1964-1970.

MATOS Escobedo, Rafael. Law degree. PRI state committee. Senator from Yucatán for 1964-1970.

MEDINA Ascensio, Francisco. Born in Jalisco. Law degree. Administrator, Department of Economy and Finance of the state of Jalisco. Law degree. Administrator, Department of Economy and Finance of the state of Jalisco 1952-1961. Mayor of Guadalajara 1961-1964. Nominated by the PRI and elected in 1964 as Governor of Jalisco for the term March 1, 1965 to March 1, 1971.

MENDOZA González, Octavio. Law degree. Justice of the federal Supreme Court of Mexico.

MERCADO Alarcón, Agustín. Law degree. Justice of the federal Supreme Court of Mexico.

MERINO Fernández, Aarón. Engineering degree. Active in PRI. Federal public administrator. Governor of the Territory of Quintana Roo. Appointed November 1, 1964, by the President of Mexico to serve out the unexpired term of the resigned Governor of Puebla, General Antonio Naza Castillo. Governor of Puebla November 1964 to February 1, 1969.

MOGUEL Esponda, Arturo. Born in Chiapas. Law degree. PRI committeeman. Senator from Chiapas 1964-1970.

MORA, Manuel R. Law degree. PRI committeeman. Governor of the state of Tabasco for the term January 1, 1965 to January 1, 1971.

MORENO Moreno, Manuel. Born in Guanajuato. Law degree. Senator from Guanajuato 1964-1967. PRI majority leader in the Senate 1966. Governor of Guanajuato September 1967-September 1973.

MORENO Valle, Rafael. Medical degree. Minister of Public Health and Welfare, resigning from the Díaz Ordaz cabinet in August 1968 to accept the PRI nomination as Governor of Puebla, for the term February 1, 1969 to February 1, 1975.

MORONES Prieto, Ignacio. Born in Nuevo León. Medical degree. Executive Officer (Oficial Mayor) for the Ministry of Public Health and Welfare. Governor of the state of Nuevo León. Secretary of Health and Welfare in the cabinet of President Ruíz Cortines during 1952-1958. Mexican Ambassador to France 1959 through 1965. Director of the Mexican Institute of Social Security (IMSS) in the Díaz Ordaz cabinet 1966-1970.

MORUA Johnson, Mario. Born in Sonora. Chairman of the Sonora State Committee of the PRI 1961-1967. Senator from Sonora filling out an unexpired term from 1968 to 1970.

MOYA Palencia, Mario. Law degree. Director General of the federal Bureau of Cinematography, Ministry of Gobernación, 1964-1970.

MURILLO Vidal, Rafael. Law degree. Senator from Veracruz 1964-1968. Elected Governor of Veracruz for the term December 1968 to December 1974.

N

NAVARRETE, Alfredo. Director of the government development bank Nacional Financiera.

NAVARRO, José Luis. Born in Aguascalientes. Law degree. Justice of the state Supreme Court of Aguascalientes.

NORZAGARAY, Bernardo. Born in Guasave, Sinaloa, on July 1, 1910. Bachelor's degree from the French-English Institute of Mexico City. Engineering agronomy degree from the Agricultural College of Ciudad Juárez, Chihuahua. Rancher in Chihuahua. Administrator for the Communal-Farm (Ejido) Bank in Culiacán and Mazatlán, Sinaloa. Administrator for the Agricultural Bank of Culiacán. Director of Farm Loans for the Bank of Sinaloa. Agricultural Credit Department Manager of the National Army-Navy Bank in Mexico City. Federal Deputy from the 4th congressional district of Sinaloa.

Representative of the National Farmer-Peasant Federation (CNC) in the National Executive Committee of the PRI. Secretary of State for Sinaloa. President of the Federal Betterment Board (Junta Federal de Mejoras Materiales) of Ciudad Juárez, Chihuahua, 1958 to 1964. Helped raise funds for public projects as Junta chairman, thereby winning citations from various civic groups of Chihuahua. Nominated by the PRI and elected in 1968 as Mayor of Cuidad Juárez for the term 1968-1971.

O

OBREGON, Alvaro, Jr. Born in Sonora, the son of former President of Mexico Alvaro Obregón Sr. Governor of Sonora from September 1955 to September 1961. Consultant on government-business relations.

OLIVARES Santana, Enrique. Born in Aguascalientes in 1921. Education degree. Educational administrator. Member State Legislature of Aguascalientes. Federal Deputy. Governor of the state of Aguascalientes from December 1, 1962 to February 15, 1968. Elected in February 1968 as Secretary General of the PRI.

OLIVERA Gómez, Mario. Born in the state of México. Medical degree. Senator from the state of México during 1964-1970.

ORDORICA Inclán, Fernando. Law degree. Senator from the state of México during 1964-1970.

ORTIZ Avila, José. Born in Campeche. PRI committeeman. Law degree. Practicing attorney. Army officer, reverting to inactive status as Colonel. Governor of the state of Campeche from September 1961 to September 1967.

ORTIZ Mena, Antonio. Born in Parral, Chihuahua, on September 22, 1908. Law degree from the National University of Mexico. Director of the Mexican Institute of Social Security (IMSS) in the Ruíz Cortines cabinet during December 1952-December 1958. Minister of Finance and Public Credit in the López Mateos cabinet during December 1958-December 1964. Minister of Finance and Public Credit in the Díaz Ordaz cabinet during December 1964-December 1970.

ORTIZ Mena, Raúl. Law degree. Undersecretary of the Ministry of the Presidency for the cabinet of Díaz Ordaz from December 15, 1964 to November 6, 1968. Consulting economist.

P

PACHECO Iturribarría, José. Career officer in the Army, reverting to inactive status as Brigadier General, PRI committeeman in Oaxaca. Senator from Oaxaca during 1964-1970.

PADILLA Ascencio, Adalberto. Law degree. Justice of the federal Supreme Court of Mexico.

PADILLA Nervo, Luis. Law degree from the National University. Career diplomat and ambassador. Secretary of Foreign Relations in the cabinet of President Ruíz Cortines from December 1952 to December 1958. Consultant on foreign relations and foreign trade.

PADILLA Peñaloza, Ezequiel. Born in Guerrero. Law degree. PRI committeeman. Senator from the state of Guerrero during 1964-1970.

PADILLA Segura, José Antonio. Engineering degree. Professional electrical engineer. Earned doctorate in science from the National University. Professor of electrical engineering, then director general of the National Polytechnic Institute (IPN). Minister of Communications and Transportation in the cabinet of President Díaz Ordaz during 1964-1970.

PAEZ Urquidi, Alejandro. Born in Durango. PRI committeeman for Durango. Governor of the state of Durango for the term from September 1968 to September 1974.

PAGLIAI, Bruno. Born in Módena, Italy, on July 3, 1902. Bachelor's degree from the Technical Institute of Módena. Engineering student at the university. Service in the army of Italy 1918. Italian-Mexican trade executive 1930-1941. Naturalized citizen of Mexico. Married to the actress Merle Oberon. President of TAMSA Steel Corporation, on Board of Diesel Nacional Trucks, major stockholder in Teléfonos de México, and the Pagliai Foundation for History Book Publishing. Consultant to the federal government on low-cost public school construction.

PALACIOS, Aurora Jiménez de. Born in 1926. Law degree. Married Sr. Palacios. Feminine Action PRI leader in Baja California. In a special election in July 1954, she was elected as the first woman in Mexico to the federal Congress as a Deputy from Baja California.

PALOMARES, Noé. Born in Sonora. Law degree. Federal Deputy from the first congressional district of Sonora 1959 to 1952. PRI state committeeman. Senator from Sonora during 1952-1958. Executive Officer (Oficial Mayor) for the Ministry of Agriculture and Livestock in the cabinet of President Díaz Ordaz during 1964-1965. Undersecretary of Agriculture for Forestry 1965-1970.

PEREZ Peña, Rubén. Law degree. Director General of administration of the Ministry of Gobernación during 1964-1970.

PEREZ Reyes, Elsa. Committeewoman in Feminine Action of the PRI. Director of press and public relations for the Ministry of Labor during 1964-1970.

PEREZ Velva, Juan. Born in Guanajuato. PRI state committeeman. Medical degree. Senator from the state of Guanajuato during 1964-1970.

PESQUEIRA, Eugenio V. Consul General of Mexico in New York City, in charge of Mexican consulates for northeastern United States.

PESQUEIRA, Ignacio A. Mexican Consul in San Diego, California.

PESQUEIRA, Víctor M. Born in Cananea, Sonora, on July 3, 1910, son of General Ignacio L. Pesqueira, Governor of Sonora and Revolutionary leader and Minister of War under President Carranza. Víctor Pesqueira graduated from the National Military Academy. Chancellor of the Mexican Consulate in Houston, Oklahoma City, Kansas City, Toronto, Montreal, New York, Los Angeles, and San Francisco. Vice-Consul in Albuquerque, New Mexico. Director of Advertising for American Airlines de Mexico, then account executive for J. Walter Thompson Advertising de Mexico. Re-entered the Foreign Service in 1961. Consul in Phoenix,Arizona, since 1963.

PINTADO Borrego, Fausto. Born in Tabasco. Law degree. PRI committeeman for Tabasco. Senator from the state of Tabasco during 1964-1970.

PORTES Gil, Emilio. Born in Ciudad Victoria, Tamaulipas in 1891. Law degree. Federal Deputy in Congress. Governor of Tamaulipas 1925-1928. Minister of Gobernación 1928. President of México 1928-1930. Practicing attorney, working to obtain abolition of the death penalty in the Federal District and in several states. Honorary Doctor of Laws degree from Texas Technological College in Lubbock in 1967. Consultant on government-business relations.

POZO, Agapito. Born in Querétaro. Law degree. Practicing attorney. PRI committeeman. Governor of the state of Querétaro. Justice of the federal Supreme Court of Mexico since 1950. Chief Justice of the Supreme Court in 1958, and 1964 through 1968. Retired as Chief Justice on January 1, 1969.

PULIDO Islas, Alfonso. Economics degree. Professional economist. Assistant Director for Administration of the Mexican Institute for Social Security (IMSS) during 1964-1970.

Q

QUINTANILLA, Luis. Law degree. Career diplomat. Mexican Ambassador to the Organization of American States, Council in Washington, D.C. Retired from the foreign service. Author of widely-read book *A Latin American Speaks*. In 1968 and 1969 active as president of the Mexican Academy of International Law.

R

RAMIREZ Guerrero, Carlos. Born in Pachuca, Hidalgo. Bachelor's degree from the Scientific and Literary Institute. Law degree from the National University of Mexico. Municipal Judge for Pachuca. Assistant Attorney General for the state of Hidalgo. Director of the Department of Economy for Hidalgo. Secretary of State for Hidalgo. Governor of Hidalgo from April 1963 to April 1969.

RAMIREZ Limón, Leopoldo. Law degree. Private secretary for the Ministry of the Presidency of the Díaz Ordaz cabinet during 1964-1970.

RAMIREZ Vázquez, Mariano. Law degree. Justice of the federal Supreme Court of Mexico.

RAVIZE, Manuel A. Born in Tamaulipas. PRI committeeman in Tampico. State committeeman of PRI for Tamaulipas. Mayor of Tampico, Tamaulipas. Nominated in September 1968 by the PRI for Governor of Tamaulipas, and elected for the term 1969 to 1975.

REBOLLEDO Fernández, Mario G. Law degree. Justice of the federal Supreme Court of Mexico.

RECHKIMAN Kirk, Benjamín. Law degree. Private secretary for the Minister of Industry and Commerce during 1964-1970.

REYES Heroles, Jesús. Law degree. Professor of history, National University of Mexico. Author of histories of Mexico. Member of the Mexican Academy of History. Director of Petroleos Mexicanos (Pemex) in the Díaz Ordaz cabinet during 1964-1970.

RICARDI Tirado, José. PRI committeeman for Baja California. Senator from Baja California Norte during 1964-1970.

RIOS Elizando, Roberto. Law degree. Executive Officer (Oficial Mayor) of the Ministry of Public Works during 1964-1970.

RIVA Palacio, Emilio. Law degree. PRI committeeman for the state of Morelos. Governor of Morelos for the term May 1964 to May 1970.

RIVERA Silva, Manuel. Law degree. Justice of the federal Supreme Court of Mexico.

RIVERA Uribe, Diódoro. Born in Morelos. Law degree. PRI committeeman for Morelos. Senator from Morelos during 1964-1970.

ROBLEDO Santiago, Edgar. Education degree. Secondary School Professor and Administrator. Secretary General of the Federation of Unions of Government Employees (FSTSE) since 1967.

ROBLES Martínez, Jesús. Engineering degree. PRI committeeman for the state of Colima. Secretary General of the Federation of Unions of Government Employees (FSTSE) 1964-1967. Senator from Colima during 1964-1970.

ROCHA, Antonio. Born in San Luis Potosí. Law degree. Practicing attorney. Federal Attorney General in the Díaz Ordaz cabinet from December 1964 to 1967. Resigned to accept the PRI nomination for Governor of San Luis Potosí and elected for the term September 1967 to September 1973.

RODRIGUEZ, Adame, Julián. Engineering degree. Minister of Agriculture in the cabinet of President López Mateos during 1958-1964. In 1965 became a diplomat, serving as Mexican Ambassador to Japan. On November 14, 1968, was appointed Mexican Ambassador to Pakistan.

RODRIGUEZ, Elías, José. Born in San Pedro, Zacatecas, on December 21, 1919. Engineering degree. Representative of the Department of Agrarian Affairs in Zacatecas. Chairman of the Zacatecas State Committee of the PRI. Federal Deputy from the first congressional district of Zacatecas. Senator from Zacatecas. Chairman of the Mexican Agronomy Society. Governor of the state of Zacatecas from September 1962 to September 1968.

RODRIGUEZ Gómez, Francisco. Law degree. Executive Officer (Oficial Mayor) of the Ministry of Industry and Commerce 1964-1970.

RODRIGUEZ y Rodríguez, Jesús. Law degree. Undersecretary of Finance and Public Credit in charge of the Ministry's loan division in the López Mateos cabinet during 1958-1964, and Finance Undersecretary in charge of purchasing in the Díaz Ordaz cabinet during 1964-1970.

ROJINA Villegas, Rafael. Law degree. Justice of the federal Supreme Court of Mexico.

ROJO Gómez, Javier. Law degree. Secretary General of the National Peasant-Farmer Federation (CNC) 1964-1966. Adviser on farm policies for the PRI 1967. Governor of the Territory of Quintana Roo 1968-1970.

ROMERO Vézquez, Claudio. Engineering degree. Army officer in Corps of Engineers, reverting to inactive status as Major. Private Secretary for the Minister of Public Works 1964-1970.

ROVIROSA Pérez, Gustavo A. Born in Tabasco. Medical degree. State committeeman for Tabasco for the PRI. Senator from Tabasco during 1964-1970.

RUBIO Félix, Lázaro. Born in Sinaloa. Vice-President of the Popular Socialist Party (PPS). Unsuccessful candidate of the PPS for Governor of Sinaloa in 1968.

RUIZ, Mariano. Born in Sonora. Mayor of Santa Ana, Sonora, for the term 1967-1970. Elected in 1967 as a member of the PAN but in June 1968 switched his party affiliation back to the PRI.

RUIZ Cortines, Adolfo. Born in Veracruz in 1890. Fought in the Revolutionary Army from 1912 on, reaching the rank of Major. Federal Deputy to Congress from Veracruz in 1938. PRI committeeman for Veracruz. Governor of the state of Veracruz 1944-1948. Minister of Gobernación in the Alemán cabinet from 1948 to 1952. President of Mexico from December 1952 to December 1958. Since 1959 a consulting economist. In December 1961 became consultant for Nacional Financiera, principal government development bank of Mexico.

RUIZ González, Pedro. Born in Zacatecas. Engineering degree. Governor of the state of Zacatecas for the term September 1968 to September 1974.

RUVALCABA Sánchez, Filberto. Born in Jalisco. PRI committeeman for Jalisco. Senator from Jalisco during 1964-1970.

S

SALVAT, Agustín. Law degree. Director of the federal Department of Tourism during 1964-1970.

SANCHEZ Celis, Leopoldo. Active in the PRI since 1940. Governor of the state of Sinaloa for the term January 1, 1963 to January 1, 1969.

SANCHEZ Díaz, Raúl. Engineering degree. Governor of the state of Baja California Norte for the term November 1, 1965 to November 1, 1971.

SANCHEZ Morelos, Rómulo. Law degree. Director of Social Security Institute for Unions of Federal Government Employees (ISSSTE) 1964-1970.

SANCHEZ Vite, Manuel. Law degree. Education degree. PRI committeeman for the state of Hidalgo. Senator from Hidalgo during 1964-1968. Governor of Hidalgo April 1969 to April 1975.

SANDOVAL Rodríguez, Eufrasio. Engineering degree. General Manager of Ferrocarriles Nacionales, the government-owned National Railroads of Mexico, since December 1964.

SANSORES Pérez, Carlos. Born in Campeche. PRI state committeeman in Campeche. Law degree. Practicing attorney. Federal Deputy, 1946-1949. Senator from Campeche during 1964-1967. Governor of Campeche from September 1967 to September 1973.

SANTILLAN Becerra, Agustín. Assistant Manager for Operations of National Railroads of Mexico.

SARMIENTO Sarmiento, Manuel. Born in Sinaloa. Career officer in the Army, reverting to inactive status as Lieutenant Colonel. PRI committeeman in Sinaloa. Senator from Sinaloa during 1964-1970.

SENDEROS, Luis R. Accounting degree. Certified Public Accountant. Assistant Director of the Mexican Institute of Social Security (IMSS), in charge of technical operations since 1964.

SERRA Rojas, Andrés. Born in Chiapas. Medical degree. PRI committeeman for Chiapas. Senator from Chiapas during 1964-1970.

SILVA García, Pablo. Education degree. Professor and Administrator, preparatory schools. Governor of Colima from 1967 to 1973.

SOBERANES Muñoz, Manuel. Law degree. PRI committeeman for Querétaro City, then for Querétaro state. Senator from Querétaro during 1964-1970.

SUAREZ y Suárez, Rosendo. Law degree. Director of public relations for the Ministry of Water Resources since 1964.

SUAREZ Torres, Gilberto. Law degree. Attorney General for the Federal District government during 1964-1970.

T

TAMAYO, Cristina Maria Salmerón de. Law degree. Married Sr. Tamayo. Practicing attorney. Judge of lower courts. First woman appointed as federal Justice of the Supreme Court of Mexico, serving the 4th subdivision or "sala" of the Court since 1964.

TARDIFF, Guillermo. Law degree from the National University of Mexico. Director of press and public relations for the Ministry of Foreign Relations during 1964-1970.

TELLO, Manuel J. Born in Zacatecas in 1899. Mexican Ambassador to the United States. Minister of Foreign Relations in the cabinet of President López Mateos from December 1958 through December 1963, resigning to accept the PRI nomination for Senator, and being succeeded by José Gorostiza as Foreign Minister from January to December 1964. Senator from Zacatecas from September 1964 to September 1970.

TENA Ramírez, Felipe. Law degree. Professor of law and author of books on constitutional law. Federal Justice of the Supreme Court of Mexico.

TERRONES Benítez, Alberto. Born in Durango. Law degree. Practicing attorney. PRI committeeman in Durango. Senator from Durango during 1964-1970. Chairman of the Senate Committee on Natural Resources 1968-1969.

TORRES Bodet, Jaime. Poet and diplomat. Graduate of the National University. Undersecretary of Foreign Relations in the cabinet of President Alemán. Director General of UNESCO 1948-1952. Minister of Public Education in the Avila Camacho cabinet 1940-1946 and in the López Mateos cabinet 1958-1964. Mexican Ambassador to France. Ambassador at large in the Ministry of Foreign Relations.

TORRES Gutiérrez, Vicente. Law degree. Executive Officer (Oficial Mayor) of the federal Supreme Court of Justice of Mexico.

TORRES Landa, Juan José. Born in Cuerámaro, Guanajuanto, on April 16, 1911. Bachelor's degree at the University of Guanajuato. Law degree from the National University of Mexico 1935. Director of the Guanajuato Preparatory School 1943-1944. Federal Deputy from the 2nd congressional district of Guanajuato 1949-1952. Governor of the state of Guanajuato from September 1961 to September 1967.

TORRES Mesías, Luis. Born in Yucatán. PRI state committeeman. Governor of the state of Yucatán from February 1964 to February 1970.

U

URUCHURTU, Ernesto O. Born in Hermosillo, Sonora, in October 1906. Law degree from the National University of Mexico, as a classmate of future Mexican President Miguel Alemán. Judge of the state court in Nogales, Sonora. Justice of the state Supreme Court of Sonora. Practicing attorney in Cuidad Obregón, Sonora. State Chairman for Sonora of the PNR (today the PRI) majority party, 1937. Counselor for the Legal Department of the Ministry of Agriculture. Legal Counsel for the National Bank of Communal-Farm (Ejido) Credit. Secretary General of the PRI. Undersecretary of Gobernación in President Alemán's cabinet 1946 to 1952. From February 1952 to December 1953 Minister of Gobernación. Governor of the Federal District, appointed by three Presidents, from December 1953 to December 1958, from December 1958 to December 1964, and from December 1964 until his resignation September 14, 1966. Now a practicing attorney and consultant on governmental affairs.

URZUA Macías, Efraín. University professor. Law degree. Assistant Attorney General of the state of Jalisco. Federal Deputy in Congress from Jalisco. Nominated by the PRI and elected on December 3, 1967, for a three-year term as Mayor of Guadalajara, 1968-1970.

V

VALDES Flores, Oscar. Law degree. Assistant Director for Administration of the Institute of Social Security for Government Employees (ISSSTE).

VALENZUELA, Gilberto. Engineering degree. Minister of Public Works in the cabinet of President Díaz Ordaz from December 1964 to December 1970.

VAZQUEZ del Mercado, Antonio. Graduate of the Mexican Naval Academy. Career officer in the Navy, to the rank of Rear Admiral. Minister of the Navy in the Díaz Ordaz cabinet from December 1964 to December 1970.

VELASCO Curiel, Francisco. Born in Colima. PRI committeeman for the state of Colima. Law degree. Practicing attorney. Elected Senator from Colima for the term September 1958 to September 1964 but resigned his Senate seat upon receiving the PRI nomination for Governor in 1961. Governor of the state of Colima from November 1, 1961 to November 1, 1967.

VELAZQUEZ, Fidel. Dean of labor leaders in Latin America. Active in the Mexican Federation of Labor (CTM) since 1938. Secretary General of the CTM since 1940, re-elected in 1967.

Y

YAÑEZ, Agustín. Born in Guadalajara, Jalisco. Law degree in 1929. Professor at the National University of Mexico 1932. Author of histories of Bartolomé de las Casas, Justo Sierra, and José Fernández de Lizardi. Novelist whose 1947 novel "The Edge of the Storm" (Al filo del Agua") set a new trend in Latin America fiction, also wrote "La tierra pródiga" 1960 and "Las tierras flacas" 1962. PRI committeeman for Jalisco. Undersecretary of the Presidency Ministry 1958-1964. Governor of Jalisco from March 1953 to March 1959. Minister of Public Education in the cabinet of President Díaz Ordaz from December 1964 to December 1970.

YAÑEZ Ruís, Manuel. Law degree. Justice of the federal Supreme Court of Mexico.

YUREN Aguilar, Jesús. Veteran labor leader and PRI committeeman. Federal Deputy. Secretary General of the Mexican Federation of Labor for the Federal District (CTM of the DF). Senator from the Federal District during 1952-1958 and again for the term 1964 to 1970.

Z

ZAPATA Vela, Carlos. Career diplomat. Since 1965 the Mexican Ambassador to the Soviet Union.

ZEA, Leopoldo. Distinguished writer and university professor. Director of Cultural Affairs for the Ministry of Foreign Relations from December 1958 to January 1965. Adviser on international cultural exchange.

Presidents of the Republic of Mexico

President   Term of Office

Guadalupe Victoria.   October 10, 1824 to March 31, 1829.

Vicente Guerrero.   April 1829 to December 1829.

José M. Bocanegra.   December 1-23, 1829.

Lucas Alamán.   December 24-31, 1829.

Anastasio Bustamante.   January 1830 to December 25, 1832.

Melchor Muzquiz.   August 1832 to December 1832.

Manuel Gómez Pedraza.   December, 1832 to January 3, 1833.

Vallentín Gómez Farías.   Vice President April 1833 to April 1834.

Antonio López De Santa Ana.   May, 1833 to April, 1834. Also President six times subsequently.

Miguel Barragán.   January 28, 1835 to February 27, 1836.

José Justo Corro.   February 27, 1836 to April 19, 1837.

Francisco Javier Echeverría.   September 22, 1841 to October 10, 1841.

Valentín Canalizo.   Substitute in 1843. Term: 1844 to December, 1844.

Nicolás Bravo.   1843 and 1846.

José Joaquín de Herrera. 1844 to 1845. Again from June, 1848 to January of 1851.

Mariano Paredes y Arrillaga.   January 4, 1846 to July 28, 1846.

Mariano Salsa.   August 5, 1846 to December, 1846.

Pedro Maria Anaya.   Substitute from April 2, 1847 to May 20, 1847.

Manual de la Peña y Peña.   September to November of 1847. Again in January of 1848.

Mariano Arista.   January 15, 1851 to January 6, 1851.

Juan Bautista Ceballos. January 7, 1853 to February 8, 1853.

Manuel María Lombardini. February 8 to April 20 of 1853.

Juan Alvarez. October 4 to December 11 of 1855.

Ignacio Comonfort. 1855 and in 1857.

Miguel Miramón. February 2, 1859 to August 13, 1860.

Benito Juárez   1861 to 1872.

Sebastián Lerdo de Tejada. 1872 to 1876, and again from 1876 to 1880.

Porfirio Díaz. 1876 to 1880, 1884 to 1911.

Manuel González.   1880 to 1884.

Francisco León de la Barra.   1911.

Francisco I. Madero.   November 11, 1911 to February 1913.

Pedro Lascuraín.   President for 45 minutes in February 1913.

Victoriano Huerta.   1913 to 1914.

Francisco S. Carbajal.   July to August of 1914.

Eulalio Gutiérrez. December 1914 to January 1915.

Roque González Garza.   January 30 to May 28 of 1915.

Francisco Lagos Chazaro.   June to October of 1915.

Venustiano Carranza.   1915 to June 1920.

Adolfo de la Huerta.   June 1 to December 1 of 1920.

Alvaro Obregón.   December 1, 1920 to December 1, 1924.

Plutarco Elías Calles.   1924 to 1928.

Emilio Portes Gil.   1928 to 1930.

Pascual Ortíz Rubio.   1930-1932.

Abelardo L. Rodríguez.   September 3, 1932 to December 1, 1934.

Lázaro Cárdenas.   December 1, 1934 to December 1, 1940.

Manuel Avila Camacho.   December 1, 1940 to December 1, 1946.

Miguel Alemán.   December 1, 1946, to December 1, 1952.

Adolfo Ruíz Cortines.   December 1, 1952, to December 1, 1958.

Adolfo López Mateos.   December 1, 1958, to December 1, 1964.

Gustavo Díaz Ordaz.   December 1, 1964, to December 1, 1970.

Administration of President Gustavo Diaz Ordaz

(As of January 1969)

The President of Mexico is elected on the first Sunday in July of every sixth year and takes office on December 1 of that same year. The federal Congress is elected that same Sunday in July and convenes September 1 of that same year. Deputies of the lower chamber of Congress serve a three-year term, Senators a six-year term. Thus, members of the upper chamber of Congress have a term which begins and ends in the same year as the term of the President of the Republic but in September, three months before the terminal date of the presidential term of office.

Governors of the 29 Mexican states, the two federal territories, and the Federal District serve six-year terms, but these do not parallel the presidential and senatorial terms.

Within each state, municipal government elected offices have terms of three years and vary from state to state in terminal dates.

Not only cabinet ministries, but many key federal government positions begin and end with each six-year presidential term.

Gustavo Díaz Ordaz, President from December 1, 1964 to December 1, 1970.

Minister of Gobernación (Interior), chief cabinet post: Luis Echeverría.

Minister of Foreign Relations: Antonio Carrillo Flores.

Minister of Finance and Public Credit: Antonio Ortíz Mena.

Minister of Industry and Commerce: Octavio Campos Salas.

Minister of Labor: Salomón González Blanco.

Minister of Agriculture: Juan Gil Preciado.

Minister of Public Works: Gilberto Valenzuela.

Minister of Communications and Transportation: José Antonio Padilla Segura.

Minister of Public Health and Welfare: Salvador Aceves Parra.

Minister of National Defense: General Marcelino García Barragán.

Minister of the Navy: Admiral Antonio Vázquez del Mercado.

Minister of Public Education: Agustín Yáñez.

Minister of Water Resources: José Hernández Terán.

Minister of National Properties: interim Rodolfo González Guevara.

Department of Agrarian Affairs and Colonization: Norberto Aguirre.

Department of Tourism: Agustín Salvat.

Mexican Institute of Social Security: Ignacio Morones Prieto.

Federal Electricity Commission: Guillermo Martínez Domínguez.

Director of Petroleos Mexicanos: Jesús Reyes Heroles.

Director of the National Railroads of Mexico: Eufrasio Sandoval Rodríguez.

Director of Aeronaves Airline: Jorge Pérez y Bourás.

Director of CONASUPO Commodities Agency: Carlos Hank González.

Commander of the Mexican Air Force (FAM) under the Minister of National Defense: General Luis Farrell Cubillas.

Federal Director of Airports: Juan Torres Vivanco.

Ministry of Foreign Relations

Antonio Carrillo Flores, Minister of Foreign Relations

Gabino Fraga, Undersecretary of Foreign Relations

Antonio García Robles, Undersecretary of Foreign Relations

José S. Gallasteguí, Executive Officer (Oficial Mayor) of the Ministry

Luis Alva Cejudo, Director General of the Consular Service

Mexico maintains 8 Consul General Offices in the United States and Canada, 3 in Europe, and one each in Central America, South America, and Asia.

Mexico maintains 31 Consul Offices in the United States and Canada, 3 in Central America, 2 in Europe, 1 in the Caribbean, and 1 in the South Pacific.

Mexico maintains 23 Honorary Consul Offices in the United States and Canada, 35 in Europe, 21 in South America, 10 in the Caribbean, 9 in Central America, 6 in Asia, 1 in Africa, and 1 in the South Pacific.

Mexican Ambassadors

(As of January 1969)

Mexican Ambassador to the United Nations — Francisco Cuevas Cansino.

Chief of Protocol for the Ministry of Foreign Relations — Ambassador José Muñoz Zapata.

Director of the Mexican Commission for the Alliance for Progress — Ernesto Ayala.

Ambassador to the United States — Hugo B. Margáin.

Ambassador to Great Britain — Eduardo Suárez.

Ambassador to the Soviet Union — Carlos Zapata Vela.

Ambassador to the Netherlands — Alfonso Cortina.

Ambassador to Australia — Roberto Molina Gabito.

Ambassador to Pakistan — Julián Rodríguez Adame.

Ambassador to the Philippines — Federico Barrera Fuentes.

Ambassador to Israel — Luis Weckman Muñoz.

Ambassador to United Arab Republic — Jorge Castañeda.

Ambassador to Ghana, Guinea, & Sengal — J. Reyes Ruíz.

Ambassador to Brazil — Vicente Sanchez Gavito.

Ambassador to Uruguay — Mario Espinosa de los Reyes.

Ambassador to Jamaica — Alejandro Gómez Maganda.

Ambassador to Cuba — Miguel Covián Pérez.

Mexican Consuls and Honorary Consuls in the United States
Consul General Offices Are Found In:

City *Address*	*Consul*
Albuquerque, N.M. 2820 S. W. Central Avenue	Luis Ortíz Rubio
Atlanta, Georgia Healey Building 1620	Roberto F. Shivers, Jr. (honorary)
Austin, Texas 330 Perry Brooks Building	Rafael Linares Navarro
Boston, Massachusetts 140 Federal Street	Jaime Peña Vera
Brownsville, Texas 104 Majestic Building	Carlos Darío Ojeda Maldonado
Buffalo, N.Y. 610 Commerce Building	Egon E. Rassow (honorary)
Calexico, California 307 Sherman Avenue	Eduardo Pérez Cámara
Chicago, Illinois 201 North Wells Street	Rubén M. Gaxiola, Consul General
Cincinnati, Ohio 3454 Whitfield Avenue	Mrs. Aria Parke Schawe (honorary)
Corpus Christi, Texas 148 Vaughan Plaza Building	Heriberto Spíndola Gutiérrez
Dallas, Texas 527 Southland Center	Javier Escobar Córdova

Del Rio, Texas West Greenwood & Main	Ramiro Peña Guerra
Denver, Colorado 410 Cochran Building	Víctor Romero Lopetegui
Detroit, Michigan 1016 Fox Theater Building	Jorge Aguilar Saldaña
Douglas, Arizona 1023 F Avenue	Ignacio Otero Arrieta
EaglePass, Texas 455 Main Street	Francisco Jaime Rivera
El Paso, Texas 206 San Francisco Street	Roberto S. Urrea, Consul General
Freeport, Texas Lake Jackson State Bank	Mason Evans (honorary)
Fort Worth, Texas 810 Houston Street	Arturo Garza Cantú
Fresno, California Fulton & Tulane Streets	Carlos Troyo Contreras
Galveston, Texas 3009 Avenue R	Raúl Rodolgo Cárdenas (honorary)
Honolulu, Hawaii 1021 Bishop Street	Ernest W. Albrecht (honorary)
Houston, Texas 503 World Trade Center Building	Luis Orcí Pesqueira
Indianapolis, Indiana 109 South Illinois Street	Charles E. Babcock (honorary)
Kansas City, Missouri 9th & Walnut Streets	Guillermo Valdez Flores
Laredo, Texas 1612 Farragut Street	Mario Romero Lopeteguí
Los Angeles, California 125 West 4th Street	Raúl González Galarza
Lubbock, Texas 203 Myrick Building	Manuel Esparza Tomás

McAllen, Texas 119 South Broadway	Estéban Morales López
Memphis, Tennessee 410 North Waldran Building	Rolando Veloz Canales
Miami, Florida 111 N.E. 2nd Avenue	Rafael Reyes Spíndola
Milwaukee, Wisconsin 229 East Wisconsin Avenue	James D. Sammarco (honorary)
Mobile, Alabama 103 South Georgia Avenue	Juan E. Petit (honorary)
Neenah, Wisconsin 964 Baldwin Avenue	Miguel Wimer, Jr. (honorary)
Newark, N.J. 48 Commerce Street	Alfred J. Lippman (honorary)
Nogales, Arizona 43 Terrace Avenue	Jorge Alcocer Carregha
Norfolk, Virginia C-o Chamber of Commerce	J. Acefalo (honorary)
New Orleans, Louisiana New International Trade Mart	Alberto Reyes Spíndola
New York, N.Y. 8 East 41st Street	Eugenio V. Pesqueira Juvera, Consul General Enrique Noguera Vallejo, First Consul
United Nationa, N.Y. 8 East 41st Street	Santiago Meyer Picón.
Oklahoma City, Oklahoma 2720 Classen Boulevard	Marmaduke Corbyn, Jr. (honorary)
Philadelphia, Pennsylvania 613 PSFS Building, South 12th Street	Angela Pérez Priego
Phoenix, Arizona 234 North Central Avenue	Víctor M. Pesqueira

Pittsburgh, Pennsylvania 306 Berguer Building	Joseph Esper (honorary)
Portland, Oregon 545 N.E. 47th Avenue	Fernando de León
Rochester, Minnesota Mayo Clinic	León F. Bahman (honorary)
Sacramento, California 809 8th Street	Héctor Rangel Obregón
Salt Lake City, Utah 122½ South Main Street	Rubén García León
St. Louis, Missouri 510 Louderman Building	Ana María Bartning Ramírez
St. Paul, Minnesota 285 East Curtice Street	Ramedo Joseph Saucedo (honorary)
San Antonio, Texas 127 Navarro Street	José Cano Palacios, Consul General
San Bernardino, California 18 Gardner Building	Carmen González Bojórquez
San Diego, California 625 Broadway	Ignacio A. Pesqueira Juvera
San Francisco, California 870 Market Street, Suite 516	Adolfo G. Domínguez, Consul General
	Horacio Altamirano Canael, First Consul
Tucson, Arizona 77 North Stone	Alejandro G. Jácome (honorary)
Tampa, Florida 516 Bay Street	Francis M. Sack (honorary)
Washington, D.C. 2829 16th Street, N.W.	The Ambassador Directs the Consular Service
	Luis Contreras Duffart, First Consul

Consul General Offices Are Found In:

North America:

                        Chicago, Illinois
                        El Paso, Texas
                        Los Angeles, California
                        Montreal, Canada
                        New Orleans, Louisiana
                        New York, N.Y.
                        San Antonio, Texas
                        San Francisco, California

Central America: Guatemala City, Guatemala

South America: Rio de Janeiro, Brazil

Europe: Antwerp, Belgium
                        Hamburg, Germany
                        Milan, Italy

Asia: Hong Kong

Governors of the States and Territories of Mexico

Entity	Governor	Term of Office
Territory of Baja California Sur	Hugo Cervantes del Río	May 1965-December 1970
Territory of Quintana Roo	Javier Rojo Gómez	1968-December 1970
Federal District	Alfonso Corona del Rosal	September 1966-December 1970

Governors of the 29 states are each elected for a 6-year term.

Aguascalientes	Francisco Guel Jiménez	Dec. 1, 1968-Dec. 1, 1974
Baja California	Raúl Sánchez Díaz	Nov. 1, 1965-Nov. 1, 1971
Campeche	Carlos Sansores Pérez	Sept. 16, 1967-Sept. 16, 1973
Coahuila	Braulio Fernández Aguirre	Dec. 1, 1963-Dec. 1, 1969
Colima	Pablo Silva García	Nov. 1, 1967-Nov. 1, 1973
Chiapas	Jose Castillo Tielemans	Dec. 1, 1964-Dec. 1, 1970
Chihuahua	Oscar Flores	Oct. 4, 1968-Oct. 4, 1974
Durango	Alejandro Páez Urquidi	Sept. 15, 1968-Sept. 15, 1974
Guanajuato	Manuel M. Moreno	Sept. 26, 1967-Sept. 26, 1973
Guerrero	Caritino Maldonado Pérez	April 1, 19 April 1, 19
Hidalgo	Manuel Sánchez Vite	April 1, 1969-April 1, 1975

52

Jalisco	Francisco Medina Asencio	March 1, 1965- March 1, 1971
México	Juan Fernández Albarrán	Sept. 16, 1963- Sept. 16, 1969
Michoacán	Carlos Gálvez Betancourt	Sept. 16, 1968- Sept. 16, 1974
Morelos	Emilio Riva Palacio	May 18, 1964- May 18, 1970
Nayarit	Julián Gascón Mercado	Jan. 1, 1964- Jan. 1, 1970
Nuevo León	Eduardo A. Elizondo	Oct. 4, 1967- Oct. 4, 1973
Oaxaca	Víctor Bravo Ahuja	Dec. 1, 1968- Dec. 1, 1974
Puebla	Rafael Moreno Valle	Feb. 1, 1969- Feb. 1, 1975
Querétaro	Juventino Castro Sánchez	Oct. 1, 1967- Oct. 1, 1973
San Luis Potosí	Antonio Rocha	Sept. 26, 1967- Sept. 26, 1973
Sinaloa	Alfredo Valdés Montoya	Jan. 1, 1969- Jan. 1, 1975
Sonora	Faustino Félix Serna	Sept. 15, 1967- Sept. 15, 1973
Tabasco	Manuel R. Mora	Jan. 1, 1965- Jan. 1, 1971
Tamaulipas	Manuel A. Rávize	Feb. 5, 1969- Feb. 5, 1975
Tlaxcala	Ignacio Bonilla Vázquez	Jan. 15, 1969- Jan. 15, 1975
Veracruz	Rafael Murillo Vidal	Dec. 1, 1968 Dec. 1, 1974
Yucatán	Luis Torres Mesías	Feb. 1, 1964- Feb. 1, 1970
Zacatecas	Pedro Ruíz González	Sept. 16, 1968- Sept. 16, 1974

Number of Municipalities in Each State

STATE	NO. MUNICIPIOS	STATE	NO. MUNICIPIOS
Aguascalientes	9	Querétaro	18
Baja California	4	San Luis Potosí	54
Campeche	8	Sinaloa	16
Coahuila	38	Sonora	69
Colima	9	Tabacso	17
Chiapas	111	Tamaulipas	41
Chihuahua	66	Tlaxcala	44
Durango	38	Veracruz	202
Guanajuato	46	Yucatán	106
Guerrero	75	Zacatecas	53
Hidalgo	82	Total	2,351
Jalisco	124		
México	120		
Michoacán	111	TERRITORY	DELEGACIONES
Morelos	32	Baja California Sur	7
Nayarit	19		
Nuevo León	52	Quintana Roo	4
Oaxaca	570	*Department*	*Delegaciones*
Puebla	217	Federal District	13

Federal Congress of Mexico

Lower Chamber; Chamber of Deputies. There are 178 congressional districts in the republic. In addition, minority parties can win party seats based on the popular vote. Thus, although the majority PRI wins most of the 178 district seats, the PAN and the PPS win some party seats. The fourth party, the PARM or Authentic Mexican Revolutionary Party, barely won enough popular vote percentage in 1967 to obtain five seats in the lower house. A minority party gets five seats for 2.5 per cent of the total popular vote. It wins one additional party seat for each one-half of one per cent of the total popular vote up to a limit of 20 party seats for a minority party.

Upper Chamber; Senate. Each of the 29 states and the Federal District elect two senators, giving the upper house a membership of 60. The two territories, Baja California Sur and Quintana Roo, elect no senators or deputies.

State Legislatures

Each of the 29 states has a unicameral Legislature. There are no state senates in Mexico. Legislatures range in size from 7 to 15 members. The term of office runs three years, and often parallels the first or second half of the Governor's 6-year term.

Municipal Government

All municipalties in Mexico have Municipal Councilmen and Mayors whose terms of office run three years.

SUGGESTED READING LIST

Politics and Government in General

Alba, Víctor. *The Mexicans* (N.Y.: Praeger, 1967), 268 pp.

Almond, Gabriel A., and Sidney Verba. *The Civic Culture* (Princeton, N.J.: Princeton University Press, 1963), reprinted as a paperback book by Little, Brown of Boston in 1965.

> Mexico is one of five nations surveyed by public opinion polls on attitudes of voters towards federal and local government.

Baggett, Sam G. "Delegation of Legislative Power to the Executive Under the Constitution of Mexico," *Southern California Law Review* (January 1935), pp. 114-121.

Cline, Howard F. *Mexico: Revolution to Evolution, 1940-1960* (N.Y.: Oxford University Press, 1963), 374 pp., paperback reprint, for Royal Institute of International Affairs.

Padgett, L. Vincent *The Mexican Political System* (Boston: Houghton Mifflin, 1966), pp. 224, paperback.

> Good handy, inexpensive guide for a U.S. attorney needing a general political reference on Mexico.

Ross, Stanley R. *Is the Mexican Revolution Dead?* (N.Y.: Alfred A. Knopf, 1966), 225 pp., paperback.

> Collection of articles by Mexican leaders. Even a 1947 article on Mexican political crisis seems relevant to 1968 riots.

Scott, Robert E. *Mexican Government in Transition* (Urbana: University of Illinois Press, 1964) revised edition paperback, 345 pp., Illini Books 1B-20.

Tucker, William P. *Mexican Government Today* (Minneapolis: University of Minnesota Press, 1957), 484 pp. A classic reference.

Wilkie, James W. *The Mexican Revolutions Federal Expenditure and Social Change Since 1910* (Berkeley: University of California Press, 1968), 337 pp. Much hard data on budgets, rankings of the states as to prosperity and expenditures.

Chapters on Mexico in General References on Latin American Politics

Chapter 7 on "Mexico" in John J. Johnson, *Political Change in Latin America* (Stanford: Stanford University Press, 1958).

Chapter 2 on "Mexico" by Kenneth F. Johnson in Ben G. Burnett and Kenneth F. Johnson, editors, *Political Forces in Latin America* (Belmont, California: Wadsworth, 1968).

Chapter 1 on "Mexico" by Martin C. Needler in Martin C. Needler, editor, *Political Systems of Latin America* (Princeton, N.J.: Van Nostrand, 1964). Revised edition forthcoming 1969.

EXPROPRIATION

Gaither, Roscoe B. *Expropriation in Mexicos The Facts and the Law* (N.Y.: William Morrow and Company, 1940), 204 pp.

A N.Y. attorney who belongs to the Academia Mexicana de Legislación y Jurisprudencia, wrote in detail from the oil company viewpoint. He cites cases which were final decisions of the Supreme Court of Mexico as reported in the *Semanario Judicial de la Federación.*

STATE GOVERNMENT

Alisky, Marvin. *Governors of Mexico* (El Paso: Texas Western Press of UTEP, 1965), paperback monograph 12.

"Government of Arizona's 'Other' Neighbor, Baja California," *Public Affairs Bulletin* (Tempe: ASU, Bureau of Govt. Research, now the Institute of Public Administration), Vol. 2, No. 4 (1963), 4 pages.

"Budgets of State Governments in Mexico," *Public Affairs Bulletin* (Tempe: ASU Inst. of Public Admin.), Vol. 5, No. 2 (1966), 4 pages.

State and Local Government in Sonora (Tempe: ASU Inst. of Public Admin., 1962 and 2nd printing 1966), paperback. Now out of print. But available in libraries at ASU, U of A, NAU, and other libraries.

LOCAL GOVERNMENT

Alisky, Marvin. "Provision for Municipal Government in Latin American Constitutions," *Public Affairs Bulletin* (Tempe: ASU Inst. of Pub. Admin.), Vol. 7, No. 1 (1968), 4 pages.

Bird, Richard. "The Economy of the Mexican Federal District," *Inter-American Economic Affairs*, Vol. 17 (Autumn 1963), pp. 19-51.

Cárdenas, Leonard, Jr. *The Municipality in Northern Mexico* (El Paso: Texas Western Press of UTEP, 1963), Monograph 1 in the Southwestern Studies paperback series.

Ebenstein, William. "Public Administration in Mexico," *Public Administration Review*, Vol. 5 (Spring 1945), pp. 102-112.

Mecham, J. Lloyd. "Mexican Federalism — Fact or Fiction?" *Annals of the American Academy of Political and Social Sciences*, Vol. 208 (March 1940), pp. 23-38.

A classic critique of the weak states rights and weaker municipal powers in Mexico.

PUBLIC AND PRIVATE INVESTMENTS

Vernon, Raymond. *The Dilemma of Mexico's Development* (Cambridge: Harvard University Press, 1963), 226 pp.

editor. *Public Policy and Private Enterprise in Mexico* (Cambridge: Harvard University Press, 1964), 324 pp.

Economist Vernon draws together the thinking of experts on public and private investments. Included is the 1960 expropriation of U.S. power and light companies.

COMPARATIVE LAW

Clagett, Helen L. *Guide to the Law and Legal Literature of the Mexican States* (Washington, D.C.: Library of Congress, 1947). Reprinted by Latin American Studies Association,

Committee on Scholarly Resources. Available from University Microfilms, 300 North Zeeb Road, Ann Arbor, Michigan 48103.

This reading list was restricted to books in English readily available to users of this *Who's Who*. A bibliography on Mexican government and politics in Spanish could run book length itself. The current listing from the book lists of the Inter-American Academic Books Center, Centro Inter-Americano de Libros Académicos (CILA), Sullivan 31-Bis, México, D. F., might be a good starting guide for those searching for books in the fields of political science, law, economics, and public administration in Spanish.

Glossary of Mexican Political and Governmental Terms and Abbreviations

A.C. — *Asociación Civil* or Civil Association, the corporate status of non-profit organizations.

ACM — *Acción Católica* Mexicana or Mexican Catholic Action, a lay organization of the Church concerned with public affairs.

AIR — *Asociación Interamericana de Radiodifusión* or Inter-American Broadcasting Association, to which all Mexican radio and television stations automatically belong en masse through their National Chamber of the Broadcasting Industry.

Alemanista — a follower of former President Miguel Alemán (1946-52) and a member of the conservative wing of the Institutional Revolutionary Party (PRI).

ALPRO — *Alianza para el Progreso* or the Alliance for Progress aid program of the United States in Latin America. This abbreviation is common in Mexican newspaper headlines.

BNCE — *Banco Nacional de Crédito Ejidal* or National Bank of Communal Farm Credit, a government agency for financing development of the *ejidos* or communal farms.

Cardenista — a follower of former President Lázaro Cárdenas (1934-40) and a member of the leftwing of the Institutional Revolutionary Party (PRI).

CCI — *Central Campesina Independiente* or Independent Peasant Central, a far left opposition group to the pro-government peasant federation (the CNC).

CNC — *Confederación Nacional Campesina* or National Peasant Federation, allied with the dominant political party, the PRI.

CNOP — *Confederación Nacional de Organizaciones Populares* or National Federation of Popular Organizations, the sector of the PRI which includes merchants, housewives, and most voters not active in the peasant and labor sectors of the PRI.

CONCAMIN — *Confederación de Cámaras Industriales* or Federation of Industrial Chambers which includes among its component members the national organizations for the various industries.

CONCANACO — *Confederación de Cámaras Nacionales de Comercio* or Federation of National Chambers of Commerce, which has for component members the various state and local Chambers of Commerce, each of which in turn has for members individual merchants and firms.

CONASUPO — *Compañia Nacional de Subsistencias Populares* or National Company of Popular Sustenances, the government agency which makes basic foodstuffs available at low cost to economically depressed areas.

CTM — *Confederacióm de Trabajadores de México* or Mexican Federation of Labor, a sector of the PRI as well as the major labor organization.

DAAC — *Departamento de Asuntos Agrarios y Colonizatión* or Department of Agrarian Affairs and Colonization, a federal agency which distributes land to peasants and helps them settle undeveloped regions.

Derechista — right-winger.

Diazordacista — follower of President Gustavo Díaz Ordaz (1964-1970).

Ejidatario — a farmer on an *ejido* or communal farm.

FCP — *Ferrocarril del Pacifico* or Pacific Railroad, whose board of directors interlock with the National Railroads of Mexico.

FCMAR — *Frente Cívico Mexicano de Afirmación Revolucionario* or Mexican Civic Front of Revolutionary Affirmation, a conservative group which works closely with the followers of Alemán in the PRI.

FEP — *Frente Electoral del Pueblo* or Electoral Front of the People, a pro-Castro far left political group whose leadership includes Communists.

FFCCNN — *Ferrocarriles Nacionales de México,* National Railroads of Mexico, owned and operated by the government.

FUSA — *Federación Universitaria de Sociedades de Alumnos* or University Federation of Student Societies, large university student group, principally active at the National University. It has both liberal and moderate political wings. Student groups at forty-three universities throughout Mexico have been influenced by FUSA.

Gobernación — Ministry of the Interior or of Government, this is the senior ministry of the presidential cabinet, and its secretary oversees federal-state relationships.

Hacienda — Treasury, the term can refer to the federal Ministry of the Treasury and Public Credit or to state and local treasuries. The term also means a large, privately-owned ranch or plantation, used in a different context.

IMSS — *Instituto Mexicano de Seguro Social* or Mexican Institute of Social Security, a federal agency.

INJM — *Instituto Nacional de la Juventud Mexicana* or National Institute of Mexican Youth, a teenage domestic Peace Corps, whose volunteer members help build and repair schools.

INPI — *Instituto Nacional de Protección a la Infancia* or National Institute for the Protection of Infants, a federal agency whose branches in each state provide free school breakfasts or lunches to impoverished children in nurseries, kindergartens, and primary schools.

JMMCyM — *Junta de Mejoramiento Moral, Cívico y Material* or Civic, Moral, and Material Betterment Board, a semi-official local group which raises funds for municipal improvements.

Latifundia — large plantation or ranch in which workers are exploited.

MLN — *Movimiento de Liberación Nacional* or National Liberation Movement, a far left group, pro-Castro, anti-U.S., and anti-PRI.

MSDC — *Movimiento Social Democrática Cristiano* or Social Christian Democratic Movement of Mexico, loosely immitative of Europe's Christian Democrats.

MURO — *Movimiento Universitario de Renovadora Orientación,* or University Movement of Renewed Orientation, a Catholic university student group, conservative in politics.

Oficial Mayor — Executive Officer of any governmental agency.

PAN — *Partido de Acción Nacional* or National Action Party, the principal opposition to the PRI, conservative, pro-Catholic Church, oriented towards big business.

Panista — a member of the PAN.

PARM — *Partido Auténtico de la Revolutión*, or Authentic Mexican Revolution Party, representing the older revolutionaries who disagree with some PRI policies. The PARM runs its own candidates for Congress but supports the PRI presidential candidate.

PCM — *Partido Comunista de México* or Mexican Communist Party, not legally recognized by the government, it still functions with perhaps 5,000 official members.

Pemex — *Petroleos Mexicanos*, the governmental Mexican Petroleum Industry, which both produces and retails oil and gasoline.

Pepino — a member of the Popular Socialist Party (PPS).

PIPSA — *Productora e Importadora de Papal, S.A.* or Producers and Importer of Paper, Inc., governmental agency for producing, importing, and distributing newsprint.

PPS — *Partido Popular Socialista* or Popular Socialist Party, follows Marxist line but in 1964 fought the PCM and the FEP.

PRI — *Partido Revolucionario Institucional* or Institutional Revolutionary Party, the dominant party of Mexico.

Priísta — a member of the PRI.

Regidor — Municipal councilman.

Rojillos — pro-Reds or fellow travelers.

RR.EE. — *Relaciones Exteriores*, an abbreviated reference to the Ministry of Foreign Relations.

S.A. — *Sociedad Anónima* or Corporation. The initials "S.A." after a firm name mean "incorporated."

S.A. de C.V. — *Sociedad Anónima de Capital Variable* or Corporation of Variable Capital.

SAG — *Secretaría de Agricultura y Ganadería* or Ministry of Agriculture and Livestock raising.

SCT — *Secretaría de Comunicaciones y Transportes or* Ministry of Communications and Transporation.

SEP — *Secretaría de Educación Pública or* Ministry of Public Education.

Sinarquistas — Sinarchists or members of a far right group advocating theocracy and the abolition of democracy.

Síndico — a municipal trustee. He may be a member of the municipal council or independently employed depending on the state.

SIP — *Sociedad Interamericana de Prensa* or Inter-American Press Association. The major newspapers and magazines of Mexico belong as individual members. Their national associations do not belong as components as in the Inter-American Broadcasting Association.

S. de R.L. — *Sociedad de Responsabilidad Limitada* or a limited partnership.

Tapado — an unveiled person, used to denote a forthcoming political candidate.

UGOCM — *Unión General de Obreros y Campesinos de México* or General Union of Workers and Peasants of Mexico, a far left, pro-Castro, anti-U.S., anti-PRI, anti-CTM group.

Arizona State University

LATIN AMERICAN DIGEST

CENTER FOR LATIN AMERICAN STUDIES, ASU   VOL. 3, NO. 3, MARCH 1969

LATIN AMERICAN DIGEST

Edited by Marvin Alisky, Director, Center for Latin American Studies, Arizona State University, Tempe, Arizona 85281, U.S.A.

Issued bimonthly during the academic year in September, November, January, March, and May.

Political, economical, and social highlights are condensed from periodicals from throughout Latin America.

The September issue summarizes a 4-month period, May-August. Other issues summarize a 2-month period just prior to publication.

SUBSCRIPTION PRICE

A subscription for the school year (September-May) of 5 issues of LAD: $2.00

Make checks payable to the ASU Center for Latin American Studies, Tempe, Arizona 85281, U.S.A.

NOTE

Volume I (1966-1967) and Volume II (1967-1968) are out of print. Volume III (1968-1969) issues are in limited supply principally for new library subscribers.

Individual subscriptions are invited to begin with Volume IV (September 1969 through May 1970).

For a sample copy of the LATIN AMERICAN DIGEST, write to the Center for Latin American Studies, Arizona State University, Tempe, Arizona 85281.